SCHIRMER'S LIBRARY
OF MUSICAL CLASSICS

Vol. 147

CARL CZERNY

Op. 821

One Hundred and Sixty
Eight-Measure Exercises

For the Piano

Edited and Fingered by

G. BUONAMICI

ISBN 978-0-7935-5931-2

G. SCHIRMER, Inc.

DISTRIBUTED BY

HAL•LEONARD®
CORPORATION

7777 W. BLUEMOUND RD. P.O. BOX 13819 MILWAUKEE, WI 53213

160 Eight-Measure Exercises.

C. CZERNY. Op. 821.

N. B. Practise each number at least 8 times in succession.

Allegro.

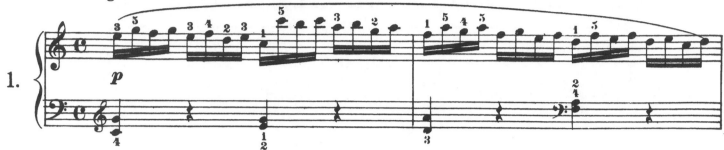

Allegro.

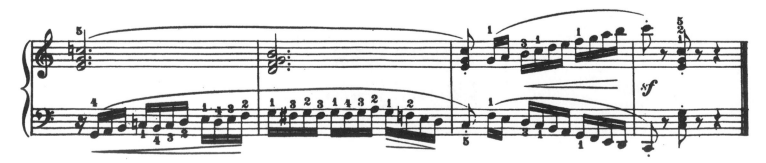

3

Allegretto.

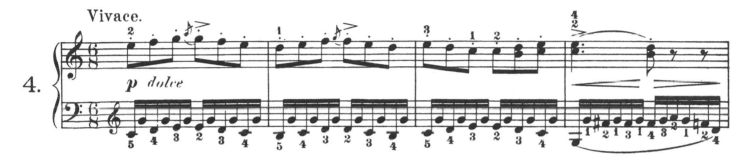

Vivace.

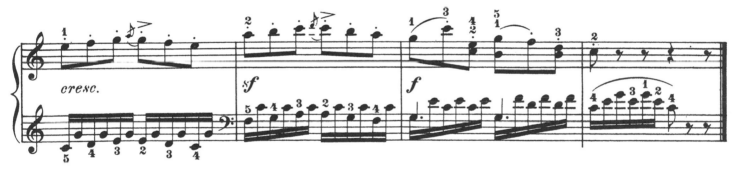

Andantino espressivo.

13697

4

Andantino.

6.

Allegro vivace.

7.

Allegro.

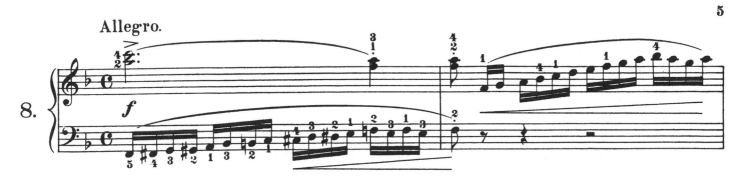

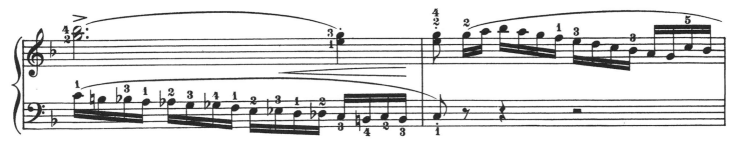

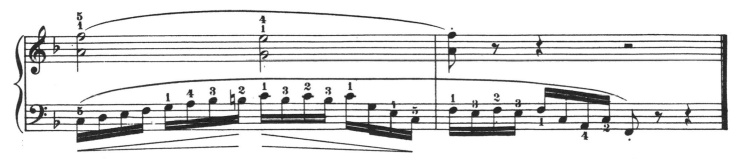

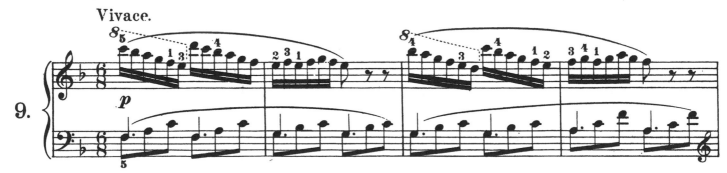

Vivace.

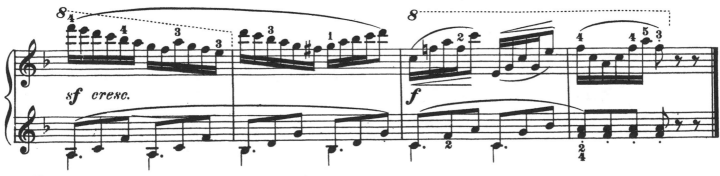

Allegro.

10.

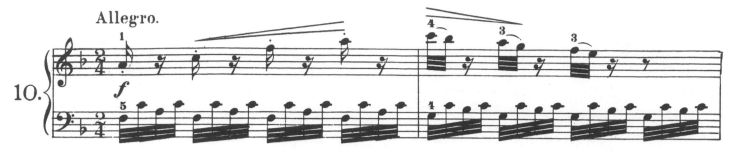

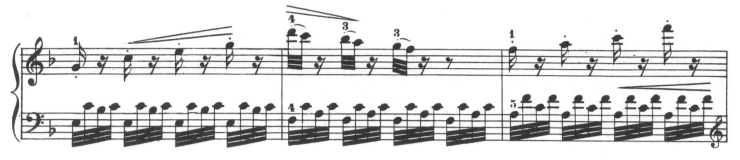

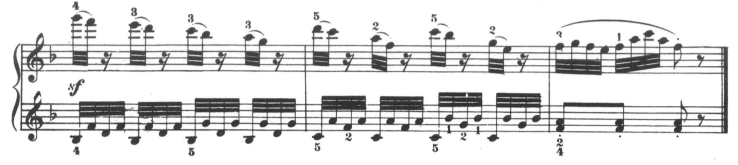

Allegro moderato.

11.

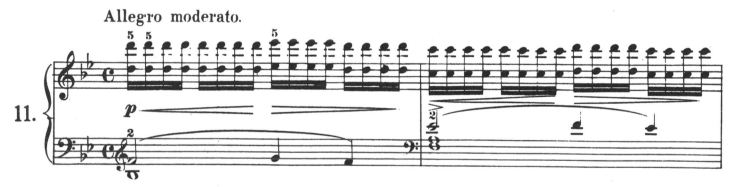

Allegro moderato.

12.

Allegro moderato.

13.

Allegretto.

14.

Allegretto.

15.

Allegro moderato.

16.

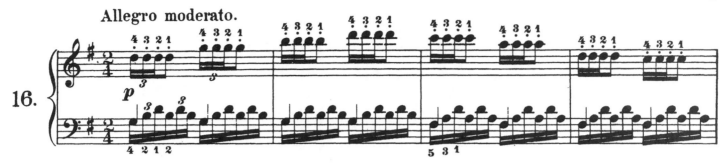

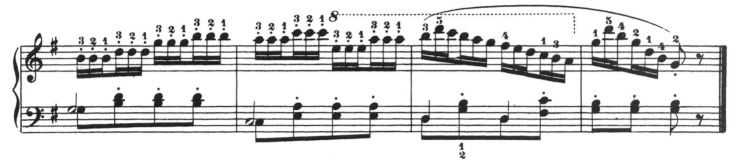

Allegro vivace.

17.

Allegretto.

18.

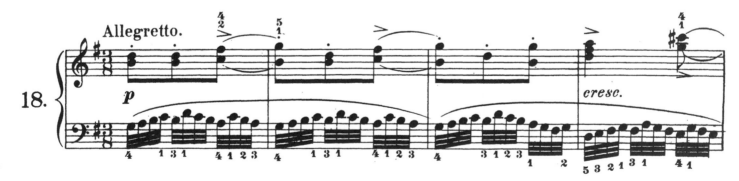

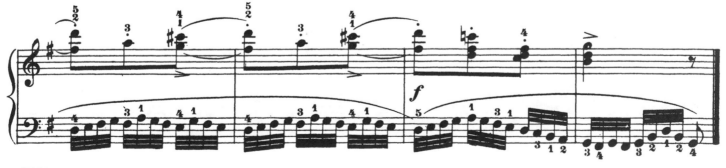

13697

Allegretto animato.

19.

Allegro.

20.

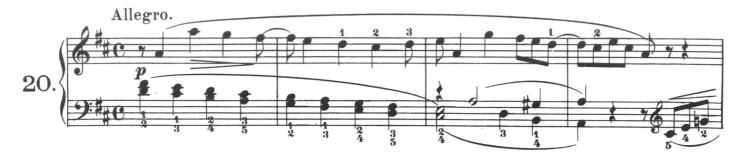

Allegretto moderato.

21.

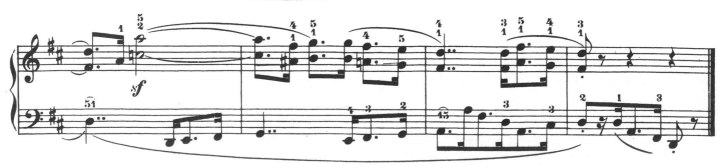

Allegro vivace.

22.

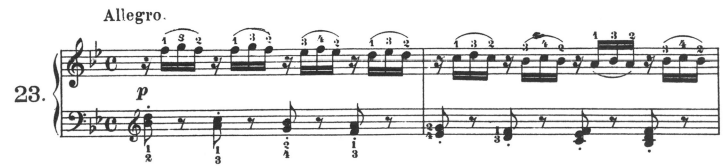

Allegro.

23.

Allegro.

24.

Allegro.

25.

Allegretto.

26.

Allegretto giocoso.

27.

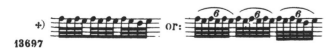

Allegro moderato.

28.

Allegro moderato.

29.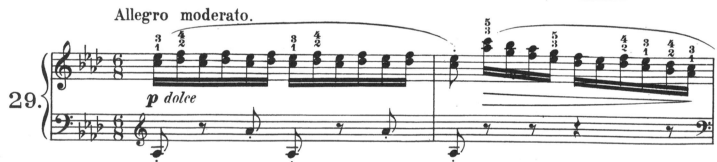

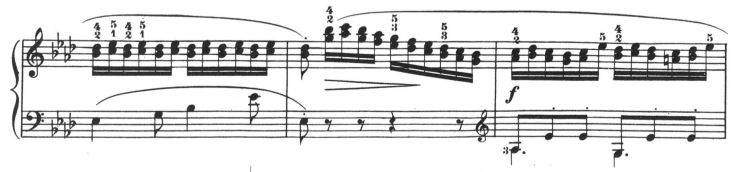

30.

Allegro.

31.

Allegro.

Andantino grazioso.

32.

p delicatamente

Allegro.

33.

f

sf   sf

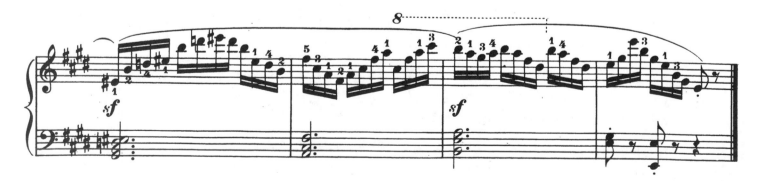

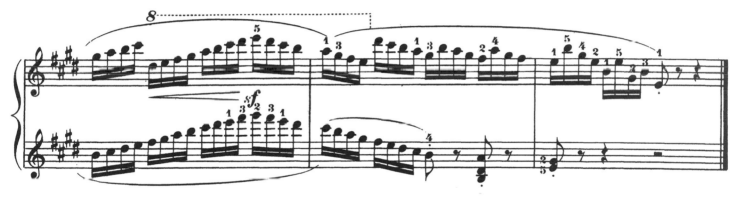

Allegro.

36.

Allegro.

37.

Vivace.

38.

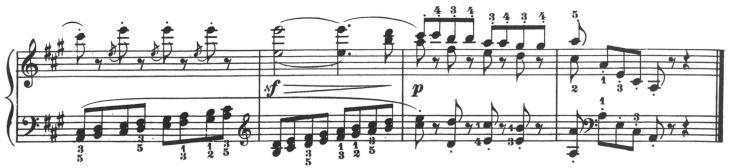

Allegro moderato.

39.

Allegro moderato.

40.

Allegretto.

41.

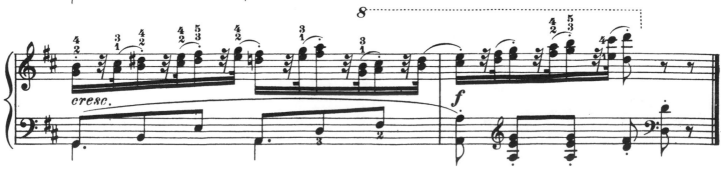

Allegretto animato.

50.

Allegro moderato.

51.

*) Perform the trill thus:

Allegro.

52.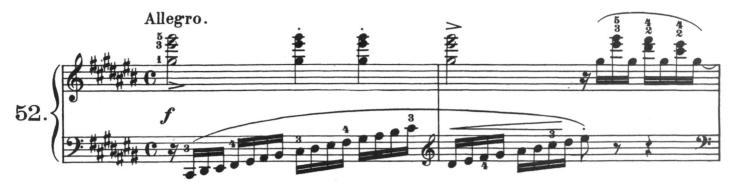

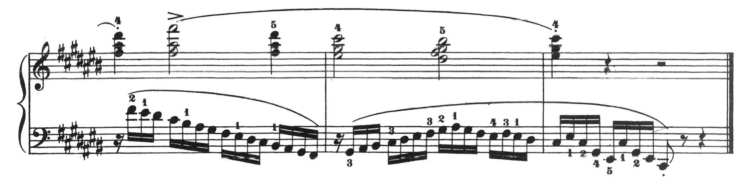

Andantino.

53.

Vivace.

54.

Allegro.

55.

Andante.

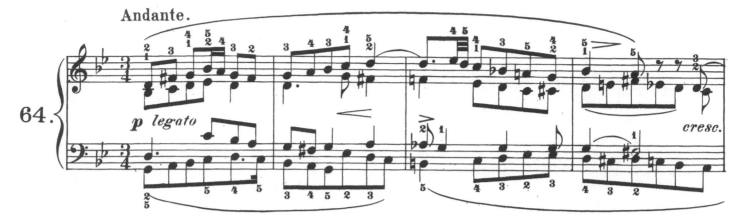

64.

Allegro.

65.

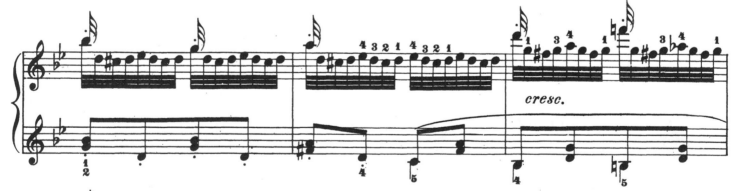

Allegro.

66.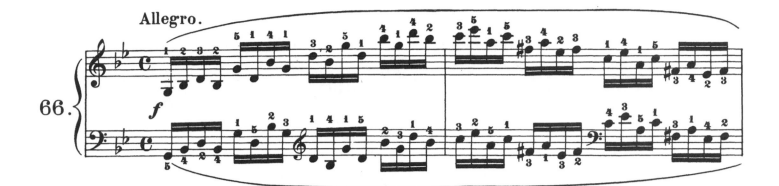

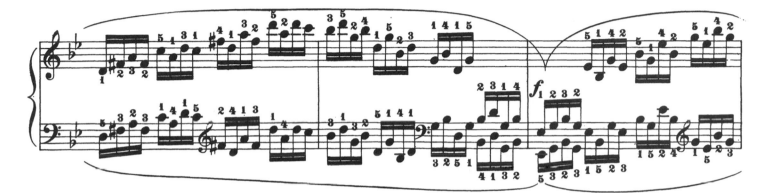

Allegro.

67.

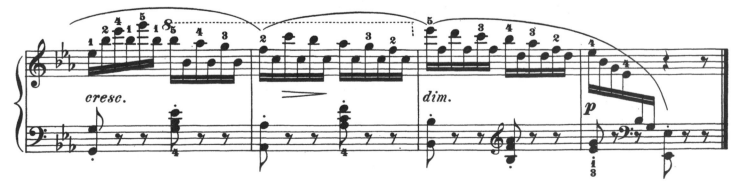

Allegro.

68.

Allegro vivace.

69.

Allegro moderato.

72.

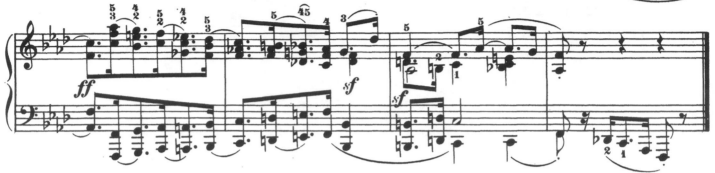

Andantino espressivo.

73.

35

Allegro.

76.

Allegro.

77.

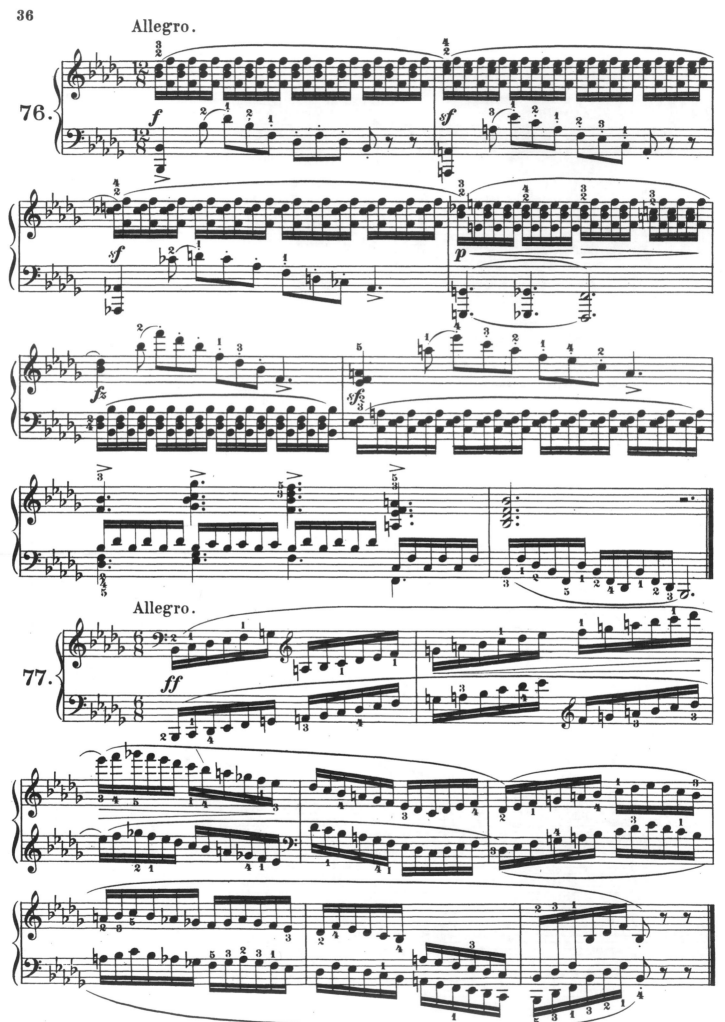

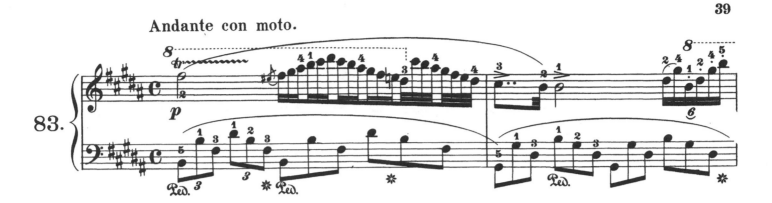

Andante con moto.

83.

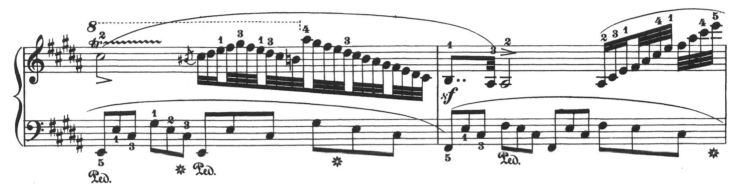

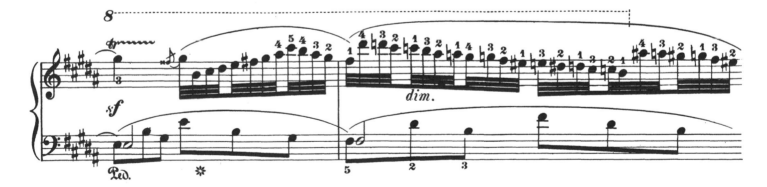

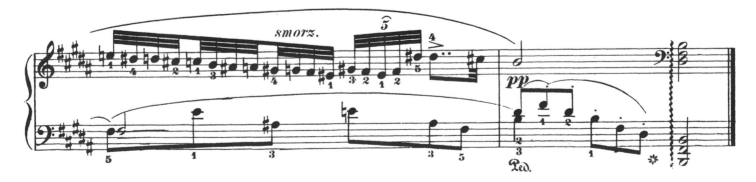

84. Allegro. *m. s.*

85. Allegretto.

Allegro.

86.

Allegro vivace.

87.

Allegro vivace.

100.

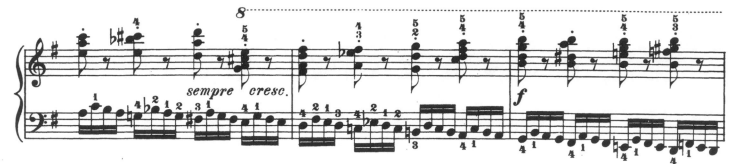

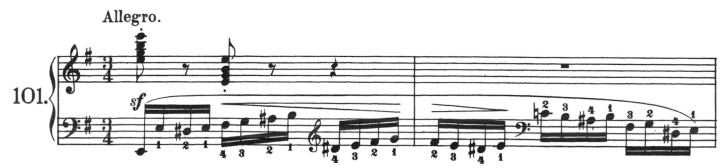

Allegro.

101.

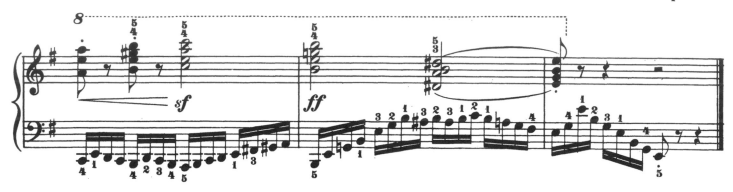

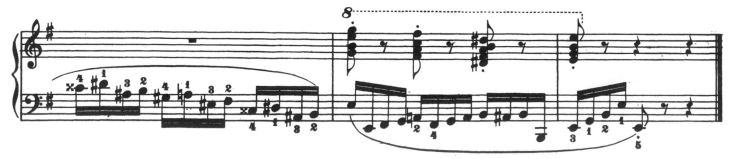

18697

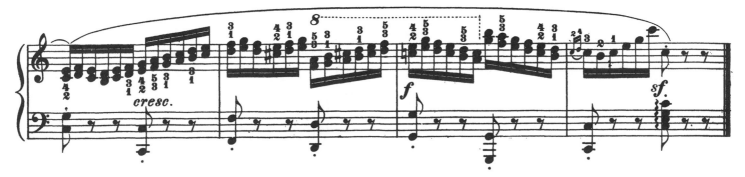

Allegro.

108.

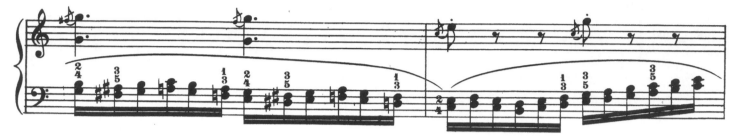

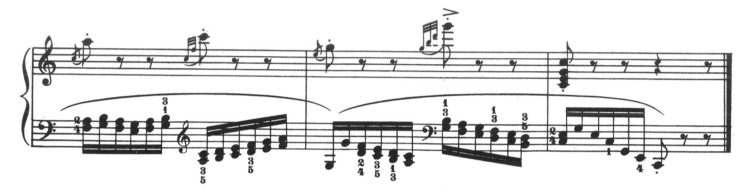

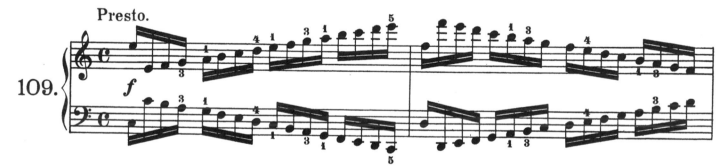

Presto.

109.

Allegro moderato.

110.*)

Vivace.

111.

*) Also transpose a semitone higher.

18697

*) Also practise in F♯

Allegretto animato.

114. *)

Allegro vivace.

115. **)

Allegro.

116. ***)

*) Also practise in F♯

) *) } Also practise a semitone higher, using the same fingering.

13697

Allegro.

117.

Molto vivace ed energico.

118.

Presto.

119.

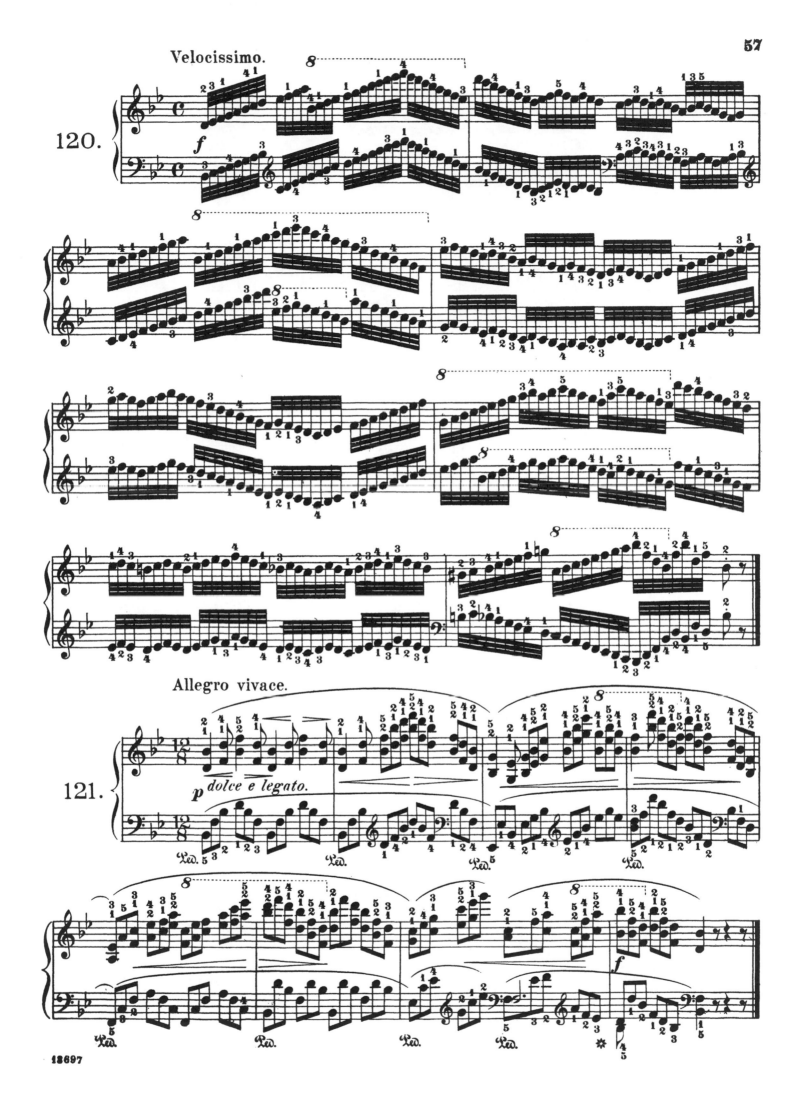

Allegro energico.

122.

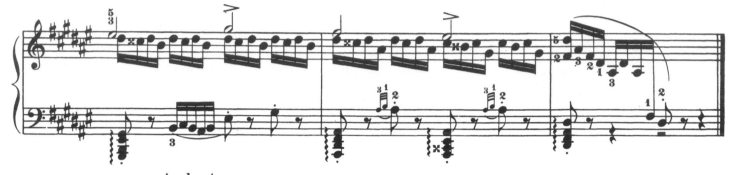

Andante.

123.

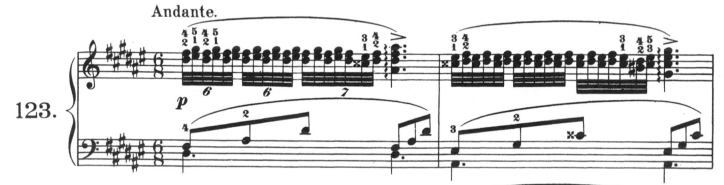

Allegro con fuoco.

124.

Allegro vivace.

125.

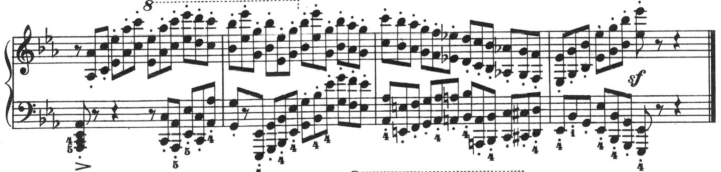

Allegro.

126.

*)
**) } Also transpose a semitone higher.
13697

*) Also transpose a semitone lower.

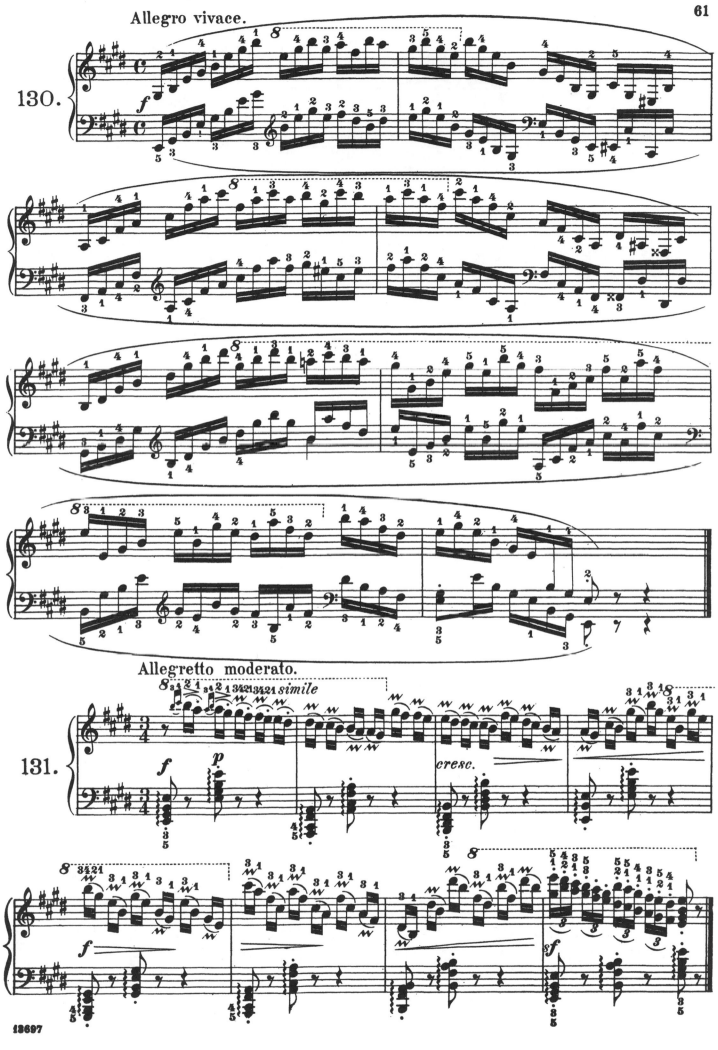

Allegretto.

132.

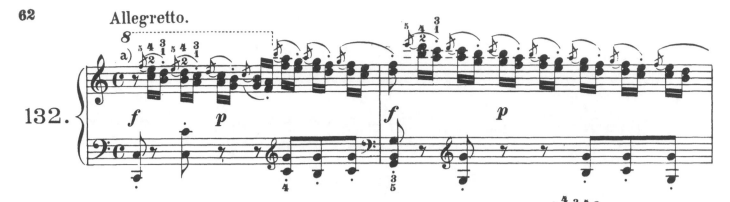

Allegretto animato.

133.

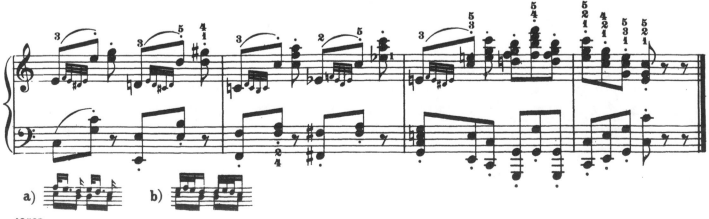

a)   b)

Presto.

134.

Allegro.

135.

Allegro brillante.

136.

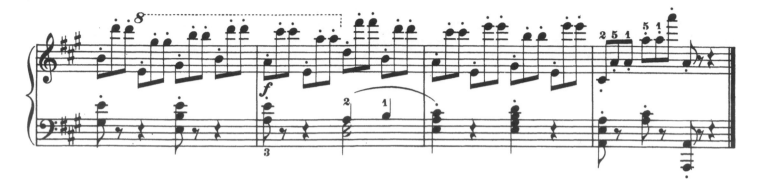

Moderato.

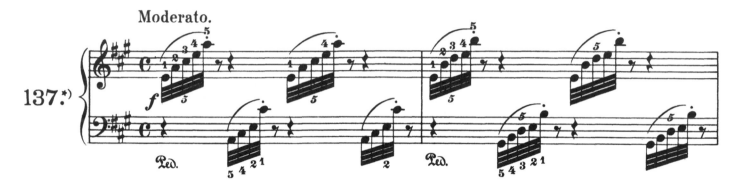

137.*)

*) Also transpose a semitone lower.

*) Also transpose a semitone lower.

Molto allegro.

144.

Molto allegro.

145.

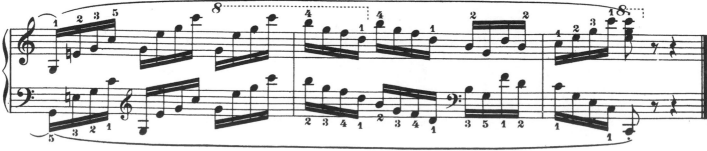

Molto allegro.

148.

Allegro comodo.

149.

Allegro con bravura.

150.

13697

*)
**) } Also transpose a semitone higher.
***)

Allegro vivace.

151.

Allegro vivace.

152.

153.

154.

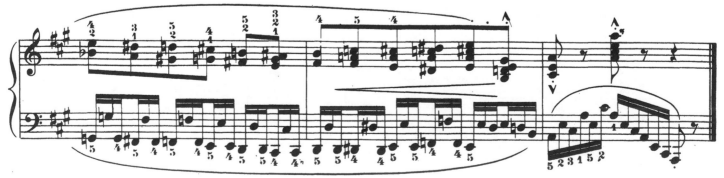

Allegro vivace.

157.

Allegro

158.